BAT
LOVES
THE
NIGHT

Greater horseshoe bat
(Rhinolophus ferrumequinum)

Greater bulldog bat
(Noctilio leporinus)

White fruit bats
(Ectophylla alba)

Common vampire bat
(Desmodus rotundus)

Spotted bat
(Euderma maculatum)

Hardwickes mouse-tailed bat
(Rhinopoma hardwickei)

Bats are the only mammals that can really fly,
and flight has made them very successful. There are
more than nine hundred species, living in almost every habitat
from subarctic tundra to tropical forests and deserts.
Birds may rule the air by day,
but bats are the monarchs of the night.

This book is about one of the pipistrelle bats.
Pipistrelles are found around the world, from
North America to Africa, Europe,
Asia and Australia.

Indian flying foxes
(Pteropus giganteus)

For Henry Venner Woodcock and his big brothers,
Alfie and Thomas
N. D.

For Ailsa
S. F-D.

ISBN 0-439-32762-8

Text copyright © 2001 by Nicola Davies.
Illustrations copyright © 2001 by Sarah Fox-Davies. All rights reserved.
Published by Scholastic Inc, 555 Broadway, New York, NY 10012,
by arrangement with Candlewick Press.
SCHOLASTIC and associated logos are trademarks
and/or registered trademarks of Scholastic Inc.

12 11 10 9 8 7 6 5 4 3 2 1   1 2 3 4 5 6/0

Printed in the U.S.A.   09

First Scholastic printing, September 2001

This book was typeset in Cochin and Sanvito.

BAT
LOVES
THE
NIGHT

Nicola Davies

illustrated by Sarah Fox-Davies

SCHOLASTIC INC.
New York Toronto London Auckland Sydney
Mexico City New Delhi Hong Kong Buenos Aires

Bat is waking,
upside down as usual,
hanging by her toenails.

Her beady eyes open.
Her pixie ears twitch.

She shakes her
thistledown fur.

She unfurls her wings,
made of skin so fine the finger bones
inside show through.

*The pipistrelle bat's
body is no bigger than
your thumb.*

*A bat's wing is its
arm and hand.
Four extra-long fingers
support the skin of the wing.*

Bats' toes are shaped like hooks,
so it's no effort for a bat to hang
upside down.

Now she unhooks her toes
and drops into black space.
With a sound like a tiny umbrella
opening, she flaps her wings.

Bat is flying.

Out!

Out under the broken tile
into the nighttime garden.

Over bushes, under trees,
between fence posts,
through the tangled hedge
she swoops untouched.
Bat is at home in the darkness
as a fish is in the water.
She doesn't need to see —
she can hear where she is going.

*Bats can see. But in the dark, good ears are
more useful than eyes.*

Bat shouts as she flies, louder
than a hammer blow, higher than a
squeak. She beams her voice around her
like a flashlight, and the echoes come
singing back. They carry a sound picture
of all her voice has touched.
Listening hard, Bat can hear every
detail, the smallest twigs, the
shape of leaves.

Using sound to find your way
like this is called echolocation.
The noise bats make when they
shout is too high for humans to hear.

Gliding and fluttering
back and forth,
she shouts her torch of
sound among the trees,
listening for her supper.

All is still. . . .

15

Then a fat moth takes flight below her.

Bat plunges, fast as blinking, and grabs it in her open mouth.

But the moth's pearly scales are moon-dust slippery. It slithers from between her teeth.

Bat dives, nets it with a wing tip, scoops it to her mouth.

This time she bites hard.
Its wings fall away, like the
wrapper from a candy.
In a moment the moth is eaten.
Bat sneezes.
The dusty scales got up her nose.

A bat can eat dozens of big moths
in a single night — or thousands of tiny
flies, gnats, and mosquitoes.

Most species of bats eat
insects, but there are some
that eat fruit, fish, frogs,
even blood!

Hunting time has run out.
The dark will soon be gone.
In the east, the sky is getting light.
It's past Bat's bedtime.

The place where bats sleep in the day is called a roost.
It can be in a building, a cave, or a tree, so long as it's dry and safe.

She flies to the roof in the last shadows and swoops in under the broken tile.

Inside, there are squeakings.
Fifty hungry batlings hang in a huddle,
hooked to a rafter by oversized feet.
Bat lands and pushes in among them,
toes first, upside down again.

Baby bats can't fly.
Sometimes mother bats carry their babies when
they go out, but mostly the babies stay behind in the roost
and crowd together to keep warm.

Bat knows her
baby's voice, and
calls to it.

The velvet scrap
batling climbs aboard
and clings to Bat's fur
by its coat-hanger feet.

Wrapped in her
leather wings, the
baby suckles
Bat's milk.

Baby bats drink mother's milk until
they learn to fly at a few weeks old.
Then they can leave the roost
at night to find their own food.

Outside, the birds are singing.
The flowers turn their faces to the sun.
But inside the roof hole,
the darkness stays.
Bat dozes with her batling,
waiting.

Bats are nocturnal. That means they rest by day
and come out at night to search for food.

When the tide of night rises again,
Bat will wake and plunge
into the blackness, shouting.

Bat loves the night.

Index

Look up the pages to find
out about all these batty things.
Don't forget to look at both
kinds of words —
this kind and
this kind.

Mexican freetail bat
(Tadarida brasiliensis)

About the Author

Nicola Davies is a zoologist and has studied all kinds of mammals, from whales in the Indian Ocean to bats in Wales. She loves to be out under the stars, watching bats, and is lucky enough to live in a cottage with pipistrelles in its roof. Nicola is also the aut. or of *Big Blue Whale* and *One Tiny Turtle*.

About the Illustrator

Sarah Fox-Davies has illustrated many picture books for children, including *Little Caribou*, which she also wrote, and *Walk with a Wolf* by Janni Howker. While she was illustrating this book, Sarah Fox-Davies met a pipistrelle in her house —it even landed for a moment on her arm!